ALONG CAME A
Spider

© Brooklands Publishing Limited
for
Renault UK Limited

First published in 1996 by
**Brooklands Publishing Limited
Holmesdale House
46 Croydon Road
Reigate
Surrey RH2 0NH
Tel: 01737 221111**

All rights reserved. No part of this publication may be reproduced, stored in a retrieval system or transmitted, in any form or by any means, without the prior written permission of the publisher, nor be otherwise circulated in any form of binding or cover other than that in which it is published and without a similar condition being imposed on the subsequent purchaser.

ISBN 0 9529684 0 1

Whilst every attempt has been made to ensure accuracy throughout this book, the nature of motor manufacturing and the possibility of specifications being changed without notice is such that the authors and publishers can neither be held liable for any changes that occur after the time of writing nor for any loss or injury arising from any of the procedures or activities described.

Designed and produced by Brooklands Publishing Limited, Reigate, Surrey

Film and reprographics by Xtraset, Reigate, Surrey

Printed by Cradley Print Limited, Cradley Heath, West Midlands

IN THE BEGINNING

So where, exactly, did the the Renault Sport Spider come from? Is it classic sports car, revamped for the 21st century? Is it bare-boned, bobble-hatted roadster made high-tech? Is it thinly-disguised racing car for the road? Is it show-stand concept car made real?

Yes.

It's a little bit of *all* of these - and then a few more random ingredients besides. Some *joie de vivre*, some Formula One expertise and even, perhaps, some alcohol! All shaken, not stirred. It's an unusual blood-line make no mistake, but then it's a pretty unusual car...

The Renault Sport Spider began for real in April 1993, following an approach to Patrick le Quément of Renault Design by Christian Contzen of Renault Sport. They spoke of many things, but specifically an idea for a specialist sports car that could form the basis of a single-make race series *and* be adapted into a niche-market road car. It had to be a *real*, red-blooded racer underneath, though, on that they were agreed, to genuinely encapsulate and apply some of Renault Sport's Formula One expertise being accumulated along with the veritable fistful of Constructors' World Championship titles.

So, this car would be suitable for competition use, but homologated as a roadgoing vehicle, too; a stimulating and challenging dual brief even before such concerns as cost and manufacture were dialled in. No matter, though, it was but an idea and - since the two men were in close accord on the spiritual inspiration of the project; the Caterham Super Seven - it seemed worth pursuing.

Just fifteen days later, a pace of progress that ultimately was not to abate, a small but enthusiastic team of talented designers had produced the initial sketches of the car that would be Spider...

"There weren't actually very many early renderings," recalls Patrick le Quément. "We were clearly focused from the outset and started with a clean sheet of paper: so aesthetically we weren't compromised, we were able to choose dimensions that best suited the car's proportions and the design just rolled down from the drawing board to reality from there, with very little reworking.

"Our aim and our brief was straightforward enough (to say anyway!): to create a driver's sports car for the year 2000,

Patrick le Quément

Caterham Super Seven

NING

ACKNOWLEDGEMENTS

Much like the Renault Sport Spider itself, this book would not have happened without the support and encouragement of a number of sports car enthusiasts who find themselves in the enviable position of actually being able to do something constructive with their 'hobby'!

Most notably, my thanks to Michel Gigou - Managing Director of Renault UK from 1991 to 1996, now President of Mack Trucks in the USA - whose passion for motorsport and motor cars was sufficient, backed by more than a little business acumen, to convince his colleagues at Renault SA that right-hand drive production of the Sport Spider was more than viable: it was an absolute necessity. The Spider is a bold car that would never have come about without such backing of those with the courage of their convictions.

I'm similarly appreciative for the enthusiasm and energy of Graeme Holt for his long term promotion of this book project and also grateful to Phil Horton, Tim Jackson and Ken Pritchard for accommodating (or indulging?) both of us.

And, finally, thank you... To Simon North for his assistance in the compilation of the Spider racer sections. To Simon Childs and Ian Kuah for some ace pictures shot under circumstances that ranged from the freezing to the bizarre. To the Earl of March and Kinrara for use of the drive and grounds at Goodwood House for some of that said photography. To Peter Gethin for giving up some of his track time at the Goodwood circuit for yet more pictures. To Brett Fraser, Gus Gregory and Richard Meaden of *Performance Car* magazine for their help with the Spider factory chapter. And, finally, to Nigel Russell, Anita Ruiz and Matthew Jenns back at base for their assistance in gathering everything together into some semblance of order.

Darren Styles

CONTENTS

	Foreword by Patrick le Quément	13
	Introduction by Darren Styles	15
Chapter One	In The Beginning	16
Chapter Two	The Wraps Come Off	24
Chapter Three	Building The Dream	36
Chapter Four	Driving The Sport Spider	40
Chapter Five	What The Papers Say	52
Chapter Six	A Question Of Sport	58
Chapter Seven	Season Diary	62
Chapter Eight	And Finally...	90
Chapter Nine	Specifications	92
Chapter Ten	Spider's Web	96

F O R E W O R D

It was spring 1993 and I was approached by Christian Contzen, head of our motorsport department. Talking in the way that car enthusiasts do, we mooted the possibility of a project that made use of some of the facilities I had available to me within Renault Design and some of the expertise he had available to him within Renault Sport.

That which held the greatest potential attraction to both of us was the holy grail that had become the quest to produce a modern day interpretation of the Caterham, née Lotus, Super Seven.

"To go faster, add lightness," was Colin Chapman's sports car maxim - and that train of thought encapsulated not only the initial ideology of Christian and I, but also that of several specialist projects we had under way within Renault SA.

We had looked at the possibility of doing a successor to the Seven as long ago as 1990, witness the Laguna concept car we showed at that year's Paris Salon, but back then the project was seen as too ambitious and, to be fair, the world car markets were running into recession so it was not the time to be thinking about short-run niche products.

This time around, though, three years down the line, the corporate mind-set had changed with the prevailing circumstances, some complementary developments were afoot and we had some key componentry to hand, too, so there was some justification in developing the prospect further. Thus the Renault Sport Spider was born.

As you'll read in detail later on it is, genuinely, a sports car quite unlike anything that's gone before. The Spider may share its basic values with a Caterham Super Seven, but there the similarity ends - our interpretation is as state-of-the-art and new millennium-ready as theirs is ingrained deeply in a glorious past. Long may both of them live!

Patrick le Quément

Patrick le Quément is the Senior Vice President, Quality and Industrial Design, of Renault SA and is the man responsible for the look and style of much of the current Renault model range - including the Renault Sport Spider.

INTRODUCTION

Perhaps the single most impressive facet of the Renault Sport Spider is the fact that Renault actually dared make it in the first place. It would surely have been so easy for somebody, anybody, to call a halt to the apparent madness of the project at any point? Innovative aluminium construction, suspension and underpinnings that are not so much race-derived as pure race car, power from the very hottest of hatchbacks, an air deflector rather than a windscreen (initially anyway), no side windows, no door handles and daily production volumes that can be counted on one hand - this is an ambitious, off the wall recipe for a product of a small, specialist car builder, not usually the domain of one of Europe's biggest mass producers.

Yet, it would seem, there are car enthusiasts in the key positions at Renault the car manufacturer - which is not always the case elsewhere - and they care not if a few barriers need be broken down in the name of producing a car dedicated to little more than the art of having a good time. The result is quite unique. Never before has any company so clearly demonstrated in a race and road car, as has Renault Sport in the brilliant Spider, the application of lessons learned in achieving high-level motorsport success.

The Spider can honestly be said to encapsulate a little bit of the knowledge gained in securing no less than five successive Formula One Constructors' World Championships - and since there's a little bit of the likes of Mansell, Prost, Schumacher and Hill in all of us driving enthusiasts then that's a happy marriage in the making. At a time when it's fashionable in many quarters to pillory the cause of the motor car, the Renault Sport Spider stands proud as a celebration of the cause of driving for pleasure, as a freedom of expression. If you don't get it, you won't get it, but at least leave those of us who do to play in peace!

Enjoy the story of this amazing car...

Darren Styles

Darren Styles is a motoring writer of fifteen years' standing, was formerly Publishing Editor of World Sports Cars magazine and now holds the same post on Autoworld, The Renault Magazine.

in the
BEGIN

IN THE BEGINNING

Ferrari Dino

Lancia Stratos

Spider

19

IN THE BEGINNING

open to the elements - the sun, the wind *and* the rain! - and dedicated exclusively to giving pleasure behind the wheel. We think the finished car reflects that, not only in its obvious track and road abilities but actually in the way it looks and feels, inside and out."

There's certainly no denying the fact that the Spider is dressed for the part of the wild roadster - styling and spiritual influences the like of the Ferrari Dino, the Lancia Stratos and Renault's own 1990 Laguna concept car having been cited by the stylists as going some way to defining the Spider *raison d'etre*. But this is no mere rework of previous favourites, Patrick le Quément again:

"Automotive styling, just like its technology, evolves. In the way that our 1993 three-seater Argos sports concept car marked the end of the period of fastidiously rounded 'bio-design', so the Spider is born of a new era - simple shapes embellished with sculpted lines and interacting detailing.

"The intention is to create a *three-dimensional* impact: the Spider has headlights that are recessed into a smooth, flowing nose but the sides and rear of the car feature a dramatic two-tone split that leads the eye-line into the aggressive semi-open rear end. And it's the same inside: do not misunderstand the bareness of the aluminium cockpit, it was absolutely necessary to convey the required appearance and atmosphere. We had to work very hard to make something so empty look right!"

And work the Spider men and women did... Late into the evening, spontaneously at weekends, modellers and engineers from the small design and development team side by side sacrificing Saturday evenings on the town to spend time in the workshop. Within a month of the fateful meeting the Renault Sport Spider existed as two models: one smaller scale, one full-size, and by the end of 1993 project partners Fior Concept were able to take moulds from the latter that enabled them to draw up the amazing technical specification.

By the Autumn of the following year prototypes were running and being wind tunnel tested and - in October 1994, just fifteen short months after development had begun in earnest - series production was given the green light. What had become a hive of activity became a frenzy...

It was a real race against the clock for the Spider team who

Christian Contzen

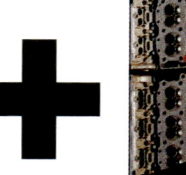 

Renault Sport F1 V10

IN THE BEGINNING

Williams Renault

Benetton Renault

Spider

IN THE BEGINNING

started work on the final, definitive clay model in December 1994, with a view to presenting a finished prototype at the influential Geneva Motor Show in March 1995. Three months of tension and no little passion followed but the deadline was met and the rest, as goes the cliché, is history...

"The incredible thing," reflects Christian Contzen, "is that the constraints of the project (within a company as vast as Renault the Spider is such a tiny, specialist niche product, remember) were always seen by those working on it in a positive light. They were given a whole raft of opportunities, rather than a pile of problems. They were subjected to exactly the same regime as a Formula One team in fact!"

Their performance is yet more commendable in view of the fact that a number of key suppliers for the Spider project, companies specialising in small production runs of complex components, had never worked with Renault before. That they, too, cleared stringent hurdles as diverse as design, manufacture, quality and purchasing with due speed of thought and deed is a testament to their collective abilities.

Subsequent Spider developments have seen the Dieppe factory begin pilot production and then series production in first left and then right-hand drive, with more than four hundred Spiders delivered to satisfied customers in mainland Europe by the end of 1996. With a windscreen in situ to offer further protection from the elements, January 1997 will see the Renault Sport Spider on sale in the UK - a queue has already begun to form for the two hundred cars currently allocated.

"We have derived the greatest satisfaction imaginable from the Spider project," concludes Patrick le Quément, "the car's overall balance continues to excite us and to have successfully combined a mechanical platform so pure in concept within such a beautiful body gives me a lot of pleasure.

"And besides, it proves - as far as Renault is concerned - that there is no longer a break between the adventure of a concept car and the reality we ultimately offer to the motoring public. Rest assured the Renault Sport Spider is *genuinely* the precursor of what we will be creating in the future."

Amen to that...

1990 Laguna concept car

Renault-Alpine A610

IN THE BEGINNING

Renault Clio Williams   **A Spider!**

Spider

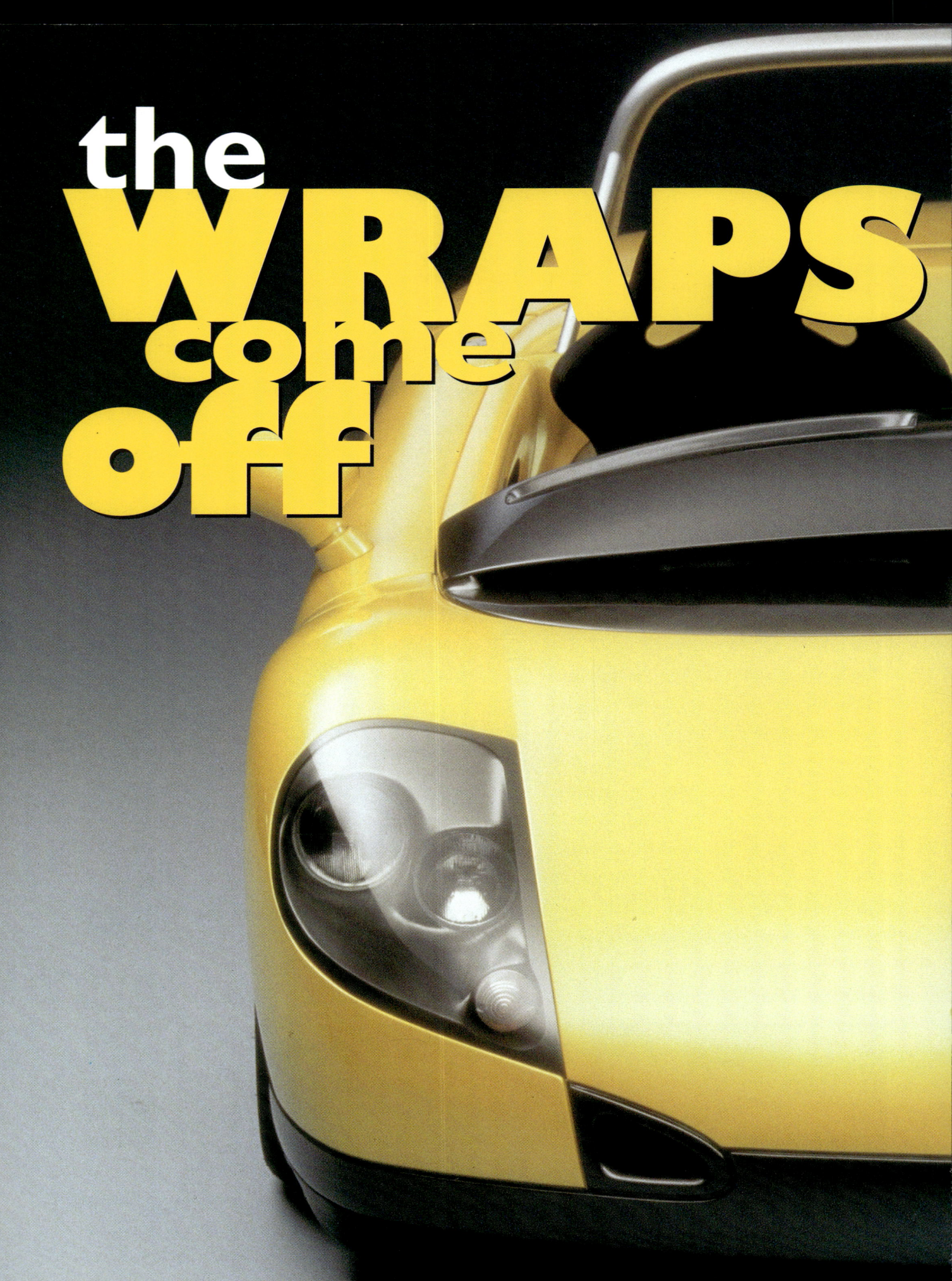

the WRAPS come off

THE WRAPS COME OFF

Even Switzerland, that most neutral of countries, and Geneva in particular, could remain ambivalent no longer. The Renault Sport Spider, unveiled at the Palexpo's annual motor show in early March 1995, was most obviously not - and indeed *is* not - a car that was going to allow anybody, anywhere to sit on the fence.

Low-slung, finished in pearlescent banana yellow and - perhaps most notably - apparently devoid of a windscreen, the squat little roadster sat on centre stage beneath the collective flashguns of the world's gathered press corps and sent out a clear message: Renault, the power behind so much motorsport glory, is back in the sports car business.

And why not? Though it's an oft-ventured albeit too rarely true motor industry fallback that 'racing improves the breed', here was a company - more so than any other - that had all of the credentials to get closer to fulfiling that maxim than had previously been the case.

A company that today has made Formula One World Drivers' Champions of Nigel Mansell, Alain Prost, Michael Schumacher and Damon Hill on the way to winning the Constructors' title for no less than five consecutive years: from 1992 to 1996 inclusive.

The Renault Sport Spider demonstrates a very direct line of synergy between that track success at the very highest level of competition and this sports car for the road and racetrack of the next millennium - it's a bold, audacious format that's easily and very obviously at least as much racer as road car. Indeed, as history records, the Spider was conceived as a racing car even before the potential of its capabilities away from the starting grid became evident.

Extremely close in almost every facet of its specification to its circuit counterpart, then, the Spider for public consumption promises the sort of driving sensations traditionally associated with single-seaters, yet without the elevated costs generally linked with sophisticated, high performance sports and supercars.

And how do they do that?

Well, for starters, Renault found itself (though not entirely by accident!) in possession of a number of specialist people, talents and facilities that offered an opportunity of the type that does not normally present itself within such large corporations. Namely Europe's most daring and creative design studio in Renault Design, a consistently successful (at many levels) motorsport arm in Renault Sport, the results of

THE WRAPS COME OFF

a painstaking four-year 'Mosaic' research programme into weight-saving processes, supplier partners (Fior Concept and Hydro Aluminium) that could actually action that research and a former Alpine factory in Dieppe that had some spare capacity as it began to wind down production of the Alpine A610 coupé. It was an impressive group of solutions that offered the opportunity to create the Spider...

Looks Aren't Everything, But They Help...

Thanks to its compact yet broad 'footprint' and limited overhangs (at the rear it's just 550mm compared to the 620mm of the already-truncated Mégane Coupé), the Spider makes a strong initial visual impression with looks that suggest it really means business. Flowing lines and curves that form

THE WRAPS COME OFF

gentle arcs are offset by the undeniable aggression of the sharp, pointy nose, air-gulping side scoops and a rotund nigh semi-circular rump that has more bodywork cut away than remains. It's a stylistic blend of true drama.

The distinctive 'beetle-wing' cantilever doors that kick up and away in spectacular fashion to reveal the broad, solid sills with integral side impact protection are both practical (making dignified ingress and egress easy, even in the tight confines of a garage or parking space) and fun - with an essence of supercar presence that announces your arrival in some considerable style.

As revealed in Geneva, to an understandable degree of commotion, the Spider was 'missing' a windscreen. This was not the work of a mischievous pre-show prankster, but rather the result of an impressive piece of lateral thinking by somebody clearly living and working in a climate well outside the UK. In fact the familiar form of a glass windscreen had made way for a strikingly-original aerodynamically-designed 'aeroscreen'.

In layman's terms this amounts to an essentially simple series of scoops and ducts designed to deflect the oncoming air (at anything up to the maximum 134mph!) up and over the Spider's occupants. The intention of employing such an aeroscreen, and debunking decades of somewhat less radical thinking, is that it will keep the driver and passenger "in touch with the elements and ensure a level of participation through feel and vision more generally associated with motorbike riding". That it undoubtedly does, but it also makes a crash helmet for anybody venturing any distance in a Spider thus-equipped a desirable acquisition.

To be totally fair, though, the meticulously-designed feature that is the aeroscreen has undergone extensive wind-tunnel testing and, unequivocally, can be said to work perfectly. Spider users are not unduly buffeted by the onrushing wind just so long as the prevailing climate is favourable...

...which is not always the case in the UK, of course, which is why, with the onset of right-hand drive production, came the fitment of a neat windscreen that blends beautifully into the Spider's lines, giving the impression it had been there from day one. Indeed, there are those commentators (and many would-be customers) who are of the opinion that quite aside from the improved weather protection the 'screen's arrival offers, it further adds a balance to the car's silhouette

THE WRAPS COME OFF

that resolves the shape anew. You decide...

The bodywork proper is comprised of a removable mid-section, bonnet lid and engine cover. These three elements (five when the doors are included) are all manufactured from resilient but lightweight recyclable composite materials of the type proven and used to such good effect in the ground-breaking Renault Espace Multi-Purpose Vehicle.

The Spider's body beautiful features an arresting two-tone colour scheme: intended to highlight the contrast between the style of the car's upper bodywork, that rises gently from front to rear, and the distinctive rear-to-front wedge of the lower bodywork. The latter element is always finished in a subtle metallic grey, but the former can be chosen in pearlescent red, blue or yellow - the Renault Sport colours...

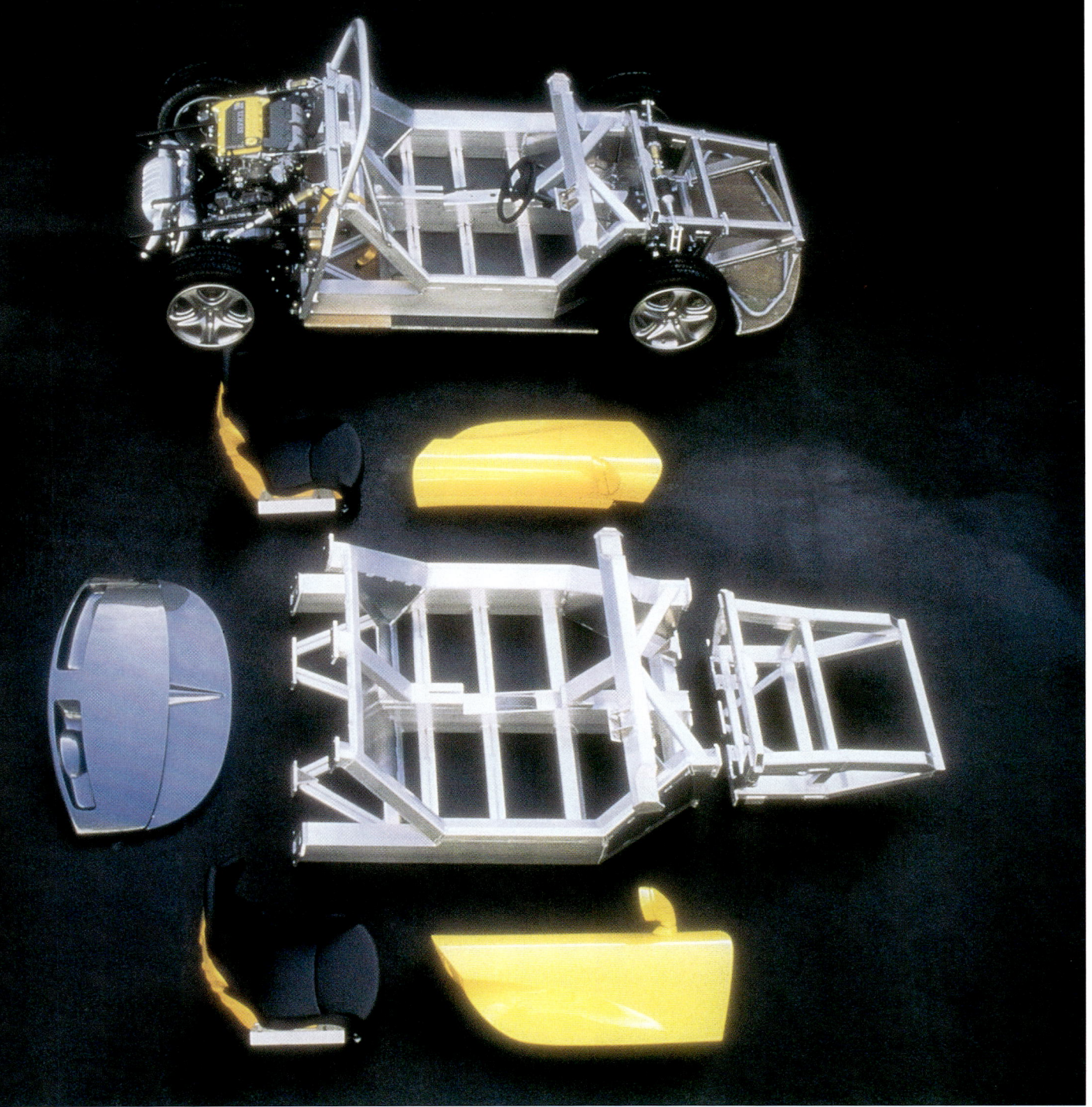

THE WRAPS COME OFF

It's Lovely Once You're In!

There's an old saying that suggests 'less is more'. Never was this as conclusively proven than with the interior design of the Renault Sport Spider.

Electric windows? There aren't any windows. A stereo radio/cassette player with or without remote control? The only music you'll need, or be able to hear, will be made by the engine sitting behind you. Air conditioning? Yes indeed, all around you. Satellite navigation? Look up, there's nothing between you and the stars. Get the picture..?

We're talking modern, minimalist and uncluttered - but no less appealing for all that: the anodised aluminium of the dashboard cross-bar and gearknob nicely offset the colour of the body-coloured interior panels while those parts of the aluminium chassis and its cross-members left exposed inside the cockpit have been left in their 'raw' state. It all enhances the simplistic, 'back to basics' feel.

The instrument layout consists of two distinct (and very different) sets of gauges and read-outs. The first - behind the thick-rimmed, leather-bound, three-spoke sports steering wheel - includes a central rev-counter set large flanked by smaller water temperature and oil pressure dials, all set into an aluminium-finish bezel. The second - located within the centre of the dash-top - houses a number of digital displays, including a speedometer, an odometer, a trip meter, a clock and a fuel level gauge. The central console houses the key warning lights.

You sit facing all of this, and the road ahead, in two fabulous race-style bucket-type seats. These offer not only the perfect degree of lumbar support but also provide as much lateral support as you'd ever need - at Silverstone or on the A1 - courtesy of two 'ears' that grip you firmly about the shoulders and torso. Made from moulded polyester and trimmed with (waterproof) PVC-coated knitted fabric in a mottled grey pattern, the seats are adjustable fore and aft and can be reclined to one of three positions to allow the driver to find the ideal position for maximum comfort. To the same end, the position of the drilled aluminium pedals is also adjustable via a knob located beneath the dashboard.

When parked, the interior of the Spider is protected from the elements - and prying eyes - by a smart, well insulated tonneau cover which can be rapidly fixed in place by a system of press studs and lift-a-dot fasteners. That's probably all

THE WRAPS COME OFF

anyone would ever need - this is the rawest of roadsters after all - but, again specifically for the UK in lieu of the likely weather fluctuations, an emergency 'umbrella-style' temporary hood has been developed as an option.

Also on the subject of practicality, in so far as the Spider provides for such a thing, there is limited in-car stowage in the form of elasticated nets in the passenger door and footwell plus a fair-sized luggage compartment (big enough for a couple of squashy bags) sited in the nose.

To protect the Spider against theft the passenger's door can be locked to prevent access to the bonnet and engine cover's remote-opening levers which are located in the door sill. As a further precaution the car features an engine immobiliser that can only be disarmed by the coded key.

THE WRAPS COME OFF

Beauty Beyond Skin Deep

As has been mentioned several times already (but then it is an *exceptionally* clever piece of design and construction), the Renault Sport Spider utilises a highly innovative aluminium chassis. It is, in fact, the first Renault to use said material for its structural components and it does so in a quest to reduce weight while enhancing the maximum possible strength. This state-of-the-art basis is a direct fruit of the labours of Renault's four-year 'Mosaic' research programme into lightweight vehicles and offers a number of important advantages.

For the main spaceframe and the front sub-frame three-millimetre welded aluminium extrusions have been used - and the results of mandatory crash-tests for homologation purposes are eloquent confirmation of the Spider's excellent resistance to frontal impact. The shock-absorbing capacity of aluminium - one and a half times that of steel - has a major part to play in that and, all told, marks a significant improvement in terms of crash resistance as compared to the performance of conventional materials.

The design of the front structure prevents the front wheels being pushed up into the cockpit while the height and thickness of the side rails ensure outstanding lateral protection. As a consequence, it's fair to suggest that the passive safety characteristics of the Renault Sport Spider outclass those of a good number of saloon cars.

In the domain of active safety, the structure of the Spider's chassis also guarantees first class torsional stiffness which plays a key role in the car's outstanding dynamic performance. From there the correlation between the car's predictable road behaviour, plus high levels of grip and balance, and its being an inherently safer car to drive is obvious...

One further advantage of aluminium over steel in automotive construction is that it absorbs engine and road surface-generated NVH (noise, vibration and harshness) far more efficiently. Though the resulting enhanced levels of driving comfort are, perhaps, less relevant in a wild sports car the like of the Spider - as opposed to a luxury express such as a Renault Safrane - they are more than welcome nonetheless!

The Power Behind The Glory

The Spider is powered by a development of the 1998cc sixteen-valve engine that took the sports hatchback sector by

THE WRAPS COME OFF

storm when installed in the Clio Williams - and is today doing much the same thing for the coupé marketplace installed in the flagship Mégane Coupé 16V. A gutsy, quick but inherently flexible powerplant, it nevertheless complies with all appropriate European emission regulations.

Maximum power output is 150bhp at 6000rpm while maximum torque is 136lbs/ft at 4500rpm, some ninety per cent of which is available between 2600 and 6200rpm. On paper that's impressive enough, on tarmac that means a power delivery that's punchy right across the rev range, from low to high and back again.

Performance levels, as those figures might suggest, are positively sparkling. All out the Renault Sport Spider will see a 134mph maximum speed (where such behaviour is legal

THE WRAPS COME OFF

and appropriate, of course) and is capable of hitting 62.5mph from standstill in just 6.9 seconds en route to a kilometre being ticked off in just under 27.5 seconds. To achieve such results you'll need to use the five-speed gearbox to best effect - again, it's the same as that used in the Mégane Coupé 16V, albeit with close ratios taken from the Laguna RTi - but it's a sensation to be relished and enjoyed.

As is loosing some of that speed when it's prudent to do so! The Spider's braking capacity is outstanding, pulling the car up straight and true in an efficient and fade-free fashion. The discs and callipers are the same as those fitted to the Alpine A610 supercar and even though the weight of the Spider is close to that of the Clio hatchback its stopping power is practically twice that of its saloon car cousin.

And all that driving hard won't see you punished at the pumps either it seems: according to UK government figures at a constant 56mph the Spider will return an incredible 44.1mpg, at a constant 75mph some 33.6mpg and around town, on the urban cycle, a still highly-commendable 28.5mpg.

Race Car Response From Race Car Suspension

Although some elements of the Spider's sophisticated suspension are a fairly common sight in the world of motor racing, such technology as they employ is very rarely used for production cars.

The front and rear suspension systems both feature bush-free rigidly-mounted double wishbones while the spring and damper units - adjustable on the competition Spider - act *directly* on the upper wishbone via a rocker arm. The front spring and damper units are laid practically horizontally and located on the upper part of the chassis. The cast aluminium hub carriers, meanwhile, are specific to the car while most other suspension parts are derived from the Alpine A610.

The rear double wishbones are of the trailing arm type and positioned in a perpendicular position to the longitudinal axis of the car and, although positioned parallel to the longitudinal axis of the car, the rear spring and damper units are activated in a similar fashion to those of the front.

The good looking, five-spoke, 16" light alloy wheels (shod

THE WRAPS COME OFF

with Michelin Pilot SX tyres; 205/50 R16 front, 225/50 R16 rear) differ in width front to rear, the latter being an inch wider at nine inches to ensure the most efficient possible transmission of power to the ground. Notably, the competition cars wear the same size wheels as roadgoing Spiders which should offer an inkling as to the levels of grip that might be available...

The Spider Gets Real...

So, from an inspired meeting of minds and talents, through an incredibly short gestation period and rave reviews once revealed, the Renault Sport Spider had a queue of eager customers forming across Europe. All Renault had to do was match thoughts with deeds and start building some...

BUILDING THE DREAM

So, the Renault Sport Spider is a racing car for the road, but just how is it put together? Rather than setting up some high-tech McLaren-esque facility (and thereby sending the Spider's price tag into the stratosphere), Renault has chosen to use Alpine's factory in Dieppe, famous for producing classic coupés the like of the A110, the A310 and, most recently, the Renault-Alpine A610. Of less interest to the enthusiast, perhaps, but more relevant to the livelihood of those employed there, Dieppe also produces the Espace MPV in somewhat greater numbers than its more glamorous stablemates.

Alpine's experience of small production runs and composite bodywork made it the logical production site for the Spider. When the A610 ceased production in 1995, workers were shifted to the Espace lines, but now they've been moved back to their spiritual home - to build the Spider.

According to Alpine's Managing Director, Jacques Martin, this highly-skilled forty-man team is glad to be working on a sports car again:

"Everyone here loves the Spider. We're very proud to be part of it and, as a result, we are a highly motivated team. The Spider is thrilling to drive, exciting to look at and it's great for us to be building a car with the true Alpine spirit."

When you enter the factory it's the simplicity that hits you. It's laid back, relaxed even, but everybody looks busy and focused on the job in hand. Until someone starts up a Spider racing car that is. It's a raucous noise and the sharp "brrapp, brrapp" exhaust note disrupts production as everyone turns round.

Walking around the airy, open working areas it's clear that the Spider is assembled here, rather than fabricated from raw materials. In one corner sit stacks of skeletal aluminium chassis, manufactured by Hydro Aluminium in Norway, and then shipped to Dieppe. In another are the engines and gearboxes as delivered in crates from Renault, while the composite bodies are manufactured by a local company.

Each Spider is worked on by a team of ten and takes sixty-two man hours to assemble. Starting with the main chassis frame, Alpine's people attach the front alloy subframe, suspension and running gear. Next the flat, plastic honeycomb floorpan is fixed to the car which can then be topped-off with some red, blue or yellow bodywork as required. Looking underneath a hoist-perched Spider, it looks just like a large Tamiya model coming together.

Once the major components have been fitted, work then centres on the interior trimming (such as it is) and panel fit. Door

Left: Alpine Managing Director, Jacques Martin, at the Dieppe factory.

BUILDING THE DREAM

hinges are tweaked here, bonnet struts fiddled with there, until all shut-lines are tight and even. At the time of our visit, Alpine had produced around thirty Spiders, most of which were prototypes and cars for the race and road car press launches. A couple of hard-worked prototypes were being poked and prodded by engineers and such ongoing research and development work has resulted in several redesigns of the French-market aeroscreen, to reduce buffeting, plus the adoption of a full windscreen and dashtop moulding for the right-hand drive cars. The roll hoop is lower now than originally planned, too, which improves aesthetics without compromising safety.

Initial, left-hand drive, Spider series production (which also included racers for the UK and European Spider Championships) began in early 1996, with the first right-hand drive cars delivered into the hands of their enthusiastic owners almost exactly a year later. UK cars can specify an 'emergency' umbrella-style hood on account of the prevailing climate, though the snug-fitting tonneau may prove a simpler and better bet.

On the subject of weather protection, though, and in light of what - at first hand - are clearly fairly flexible construction methods, might there be a possiblity of a fixedhead Spider in the years to come we wondered aloud at the end of the factory tour? After all, the aluminium chassis could easily be used as a platform for a small, two-seater Coupé, as the 1996 Geneva motor show concept car - the Fiftie - has shown.

Seems the Alpine factory may be building our dreams for a while yet...

DRIVING the spider

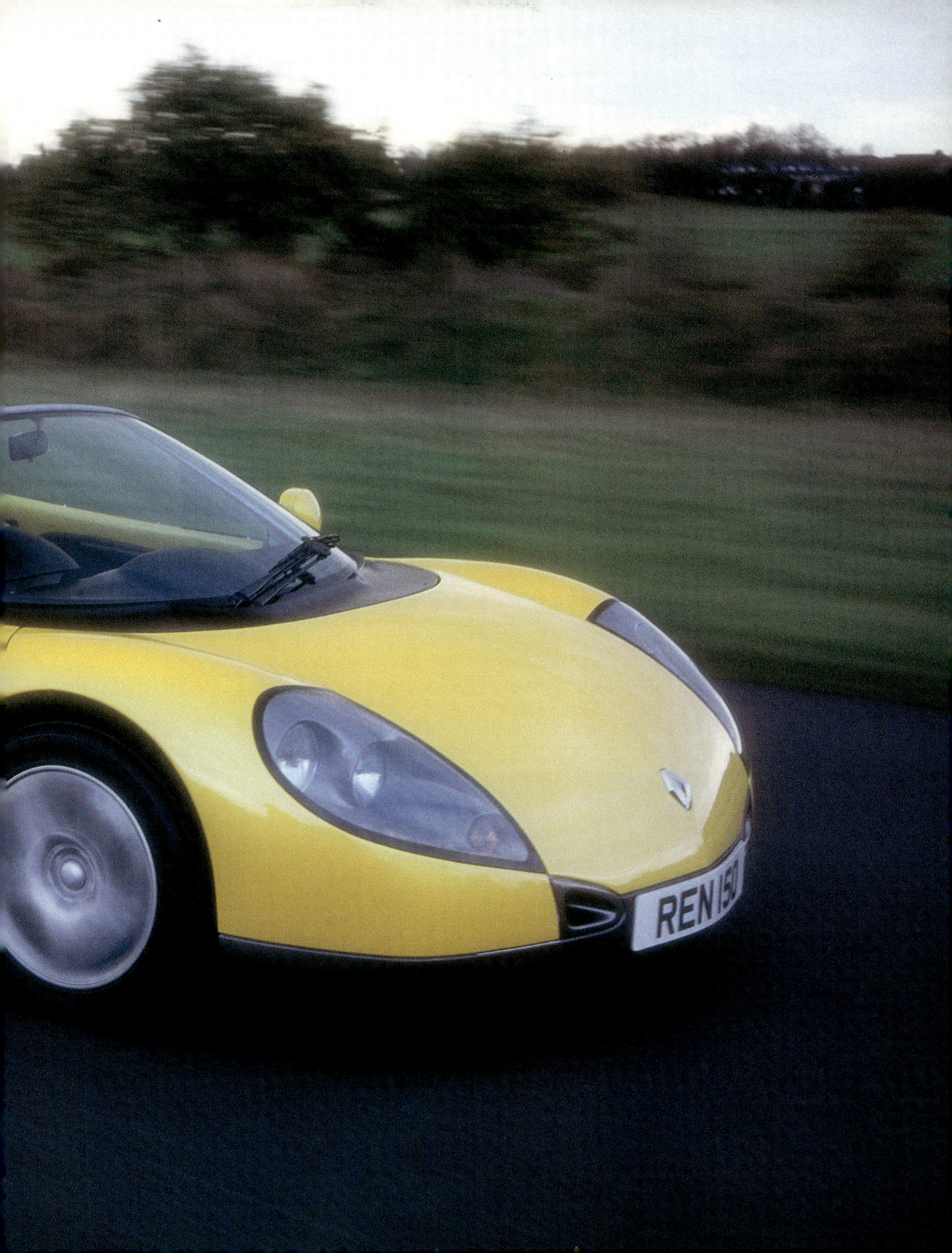
REN 150

DRIVING THE SPIDER

Bob Monkhouse, on hearing that a new generation of younger comedians (as indeed most are in comparison to the veteran funnyman) considered him to be a cult figure, imagined he had misheard. Similarly, when the new Renault Sport Spider is described as an *open* sports car you, too, will not be hearing what you think you're hearing. Because, in the way that Bob's gags are funnier and cleverer than they may at first seem (and possibly newer), the Sport Spider is even more open than the initial description suggests.

As even the most cursory glance at the pictures of this most radical of roadsters will reveal, this mid-engined, two-litre 16V-powered sports car is exceptionally bereft of any protection from the elements. Sure, there's no roof. But then most proper sports cars, in the traditional sense of the word, have no roof.

Yet there are no side or rear windows either. And though lots of sports or leisure vehicles have prospered without glass to West or East of their occupants, few have had so little as the baby-windscreened Spider in the straight-ahead direction. Or, to be more precise in the case of the European-market left-hand drive cars, absolutely none at all. So what does this mean? Why is this incredible, nay startling, little car so unfinished from the waist up?

Well, if you have to ask I'd venture you've missed the point. If you don't get it, then you won't get it. At all. Not ever. Not even for the £25,950 that the Sport Spider sells for in the UK, Oh yes, you'd better believe it; this apparent refugee from another part of the time and space continuum *is* real...

Marseille, France, February 1996, Sans Windscreen...

Marseille in early February 1996 was freezing. More than freezing point of fact: it was so cold it couldn't snow. This was unusual - the temperatures were a record low for the time of year. And I was about to get my first drive in a (rather exposed) roadgoing Renault Sport Spider. It seemed the only tan likely to be picked up on this particular visit to the Cote d'Azur was going to be from a bottle - so we're back to the Bob Monkhouse routine then!

Seriously, though (folks), I shan't even begin to suggest that anything the weather did was going to detract from the long-awaited virgin Spider moment. From the minute the wraps came off the car at the Geneva motor show little more than a year before, enthusiasts Europe-wide had been anticipating the drop across the broad sills and into that snug-as-a-bug cockpit. I was one of them and couldn't wait to get at it, rain (or snow) or shine.

I'll spare you the details of the greasy bits and how they work in situ until a bit later on, but what you must know now, if not sooner, is this: the

42

DRIVING THE SPIDER

Renault Sport Spider is absolutely everything anyone could ever have hoped it would be - and then some. It goes, stops, handles, grips, feels and sounds like nothing at all on planet earth: it's motoring in its absolute rawest form.

I'll do the equivalent of cutting to the chase scene, so picture this. I've climbed aboard, fired up, left the garage of assembled press corps with grown-up levels of dignity and aplomb in front of the assembled Renault personnel. Until I'm out of sight.

Then snick and bam: pull the palm-sized silver ball atop the short-throw gearlever back into second and mash the drilled accelerator pedal to the bare aluminium floor...

Revs build quickly, such is the eager beaver nature of the revvy 2.0-litre, sixteen-valve powerplant we've come to know and love in the hottest of hot hatchbacks, though the sparkling rise and thrum of the engine note goes on behind you in the main and gets carried away in the airstream. But most obvious of all, along with the impression of fast-increasing road speed (enhanced by the close proximity of your bottom to the fast-moving floor), is a rapidly growing sensation of wind speed.

The dead clever series of scoops and ducts purporting to be a wind deflector that sits where a windscreen should be, *does*, indeed, make a decent fist of pushing the onrushing air

DRIVING THE SPIDER

44

Spider

DRIVING THE SPIDER

over your head it has to be said. But (and there's always a but isn't there?) 'you canna change the laws of physics' as Trekkie fans will know - and the buffeting from the sides and the hissing and whistling of the ebb and flow of the wind are right there, right in your face.

And you know what? It matters not one jot, whatever the prevailing climate. Not even almost. This sensation of not just watching the world go by but actually taking part in it; feeling it, breathing it, living it, confirm the Spider's very *raison d'etre*.

There's a race car for the road under this space age construction which means you can make the very most of the considerable on-road abilities this car makes available to the skilled, press-on driver what's more. Yet each and every sensation the Spider allows you to generate with your inputs will be fed back straight from the box. No colouring, no preservatives, just undiluted sports car fun: a first-rate whizz with no Es required!

Have I been out in the fresh air too long? Gone just a little bit bonkers on the car having had so much oxygen forced into me at speed? Absolutely. Even with the recommended crash helmet perched upon the bone dome - it's not a legal requirement, but the visor does have the advantage of keeping grit from the eyes and wayward stones off the bonce - there's enough going on around you to get completely and utterly high on life.

I shall remember forever my route by Renault Sport Spider through and over the mountains that look down on Marseille and run along the coast. Brilliant blue sky, bright sunshine, brand new billiard table-smooth road surface, little or no traffic, challenging hairpins and switchbacks that made up every turn. No matter that the air temperature could have halved Mr Findus' overheads at a stroke, I'd not have swapped my seat for one at a fireside for any money. Well, perhaps that's not strictly true, but it would need to be a pretty substantial cash sum - let's call it £25,950 in round figures..!

DRIVING THE SPIDER

Back at Renault Sport base my rampant, ruddy-cheeked enthusiasm was well received. A small (no, tiny), dedicated team of designers and engineers from across the whole sphere of Renault's competition and manufacturing activities wanted to hear what I had to say. I was flattered, of course, but don't run away with the idea that my opinion mattered any more than the next man. It's just that after the Spider's incredibly short design and homologation period of only fifteen months, the UK journalists that made up our group were the first 'outsiders' to drive the Spider. How did it feel? Did I enjoy it? Was it too blustery? All told, was the car as good as they thought it was, they wondered? With Anglo-Saxon expletives deleted the general gist was yes, chaps, I think it's probably alright...

Now I had a few questions for them. Like why was a volume manufacturer like Renault building an ultra-specialist car like the Spider?

Because it can, came the reply! The thinking was simple: as the power behind some of the world's most successful racing cars at a multitude of levels (Formula One, Formula Three, Formula Renault Sport), why not adapt that expertise into a sort of single-seater for two? Hence work began in earnest as recently as December 1994 on a thoroughly modern sports car intended to utilise the very best of the not inconsiderable talents Renault had available.

First stop was Fior Concepts for assistance with the development of a new and innovative aluminium chassis. A light, strong structure, the Spider's underpinnings reflect Renault's four years of research on the 'Mosaic' programme: set up to investigate the design and manufacture of lighter vehicles. Bearing first fruit of those labours, the new sports car has fared exceptionally well in crash testing, out-performing many saloon cars in a graphic demonstration of the greater impact-absorbing capacity of aluminium - some one and a half times that of steel.

On to this exceptionally rigid framework are hung a proven set of competition-derived mechanicals, most notably the aforementioned Mégane Coupé 16V power unit, derived from the Clio Williams. Offering power and torque in abundance, and driving through a five-speed gearbox culled from the Mégane Coupé 16V with a set of Laguna RTi ratios, this strong, willing engine sees the Spider from 0-62mph in 6.9 seconds and on to a maximum speed of nearly 135mph. Those are serious performance credentials in a car close to the weight of a Clio, which is why the braking system (unquestionably efficient and totally fade free) is carried over from the late Alpine A610 supercar.

Perhaps, though, the most remarkable underskin facet of the Renault Sport Spider, and the primary reason its on road behaviour is so communicative and just so downright

DRIVING THE SPIDER

immediate, is the wholesale adoption of a set of suspension parts that are pure racing technology. Bush-free, rigidly-mounted double wishbones hang off front and rear with spring and damper units that act directly on the upper wishbone via a rocker arm. The hub carriers are cast aluminium and specific to this car while practically everything else that isn't has again been carried over from the A610.

Contact with terra firma (rarely broken under anything but the most extreme circumstances) comes via a set of handsome, sixteen-inch light alloy wheels that differ in size from front to rear (eight inches wide at the front, a still broader nine inches at the rear), shod with gratifyingly sticky Michelin Pilot rubber (205/50 R16 front, 225/50 R16 rear).

The upshot is a failsafe set of on-road responses that anyone, regardless of experience, can go out, use and enjoy. There's power enough to go quickly, very quickly in fact, but not so much that it will flatter to deceive the unruly. To get the most from the Spider driving experience you actually have to contribute: via unassisted steering and brakes that deliver unabated feedback harking back to sportsters that did more than ruffle the carefully-formed bouffant hairstyles of the boulevardiers.

And if all of that sounds a bit too much like hard work to you - which it isn't, but who am I to offer free psycho-analysis

DRIVING THE SPIDER

DRIVING THE SPIDER

- then simply park the Renault Sport Spider on the drive, sit back and just look at it. Soak up the madcap lines and wonder at the daring of the manufacturer that risked building a car that looks like this. From the tip of its low, pointy nose, over the revolutionary aeroscreen, past the 'beetle-wing' cantilever doors, through an interior that redefines spartan as an art form to a rounded rump, this car is nothing if not different. It's built for pleasure, built for leisure, nothing else matters.

In summary, and I apologise for the cliché, the Renault Sport Spider is just the most fun you can have with your clothes on. And, in the right conditions, you'd not need too many of those either. Come to think of it, buy one and drive it naked. The Spider is so wild, so wacky and so utterly, utterly mad nobody would notice. Even if you are Cindy Crawford or a Chippendale. Or Bob Monkhouse.

Goodwood, England, November 1996, Through The Looking Glass...

Ten months on from Marseille, having successfully circumnavigated the warm summer months, I am back in the cockpit of a Renault Sport Spider. Nothing much has changed. It's still a snug fit, the driving position remains tailor-made, even for a six-footer like myself, and - best of all - the rubberised upholstery proves comfy, nice to the touch and, most importantly, completely waterproof.

But there *are* two small but significant changes in the status quo - and *vive le difference*! Firstly, where previously a passenger sat propped (slightly nervously perhaps) in the airstream, the driver now finds a place to call his own. We're talking right-hand drive, of course, and as a native of England that means I do not now inadvertently open the door when intending to change gear.

Secondly, and as a measure of just how far Renault are prepared to go in a bid to make a success of their wild

DRIVING THE SPIDER

roadster in the country that lays claim to being the spiritual home of the sports car, the Spider has been adapted for 'over here' with the addition of a rakishly-profiled windscreen. And it's no mere pane of Everest's finest either, but rather a gracefully-formed arc impregnated with heater elements, finished off with a pair of the smallest, cutest sidescreens you ever saw and kept clear by a large pantograph wiper culled from Renault's Twingo baby-hatch.

All of this requires a new dashtop moulding to fill the space where once was an aeroscreen, duly accomplished with some style, and the overall impression when ensconced in a UK-specification Spider is one of a still-crazy-after-all-these-years sports car that has done little but mature a modicum, thanks to a little added practicality.

Has this diluted the Renault Sport Spider's appeal you may wonder? With the passing of the wind in the hair, flies in the teeth, stone chips in the retina aeroscreen has a little of the Spider's soul gone missing? In a word: no. Indeed, notwithstanding the popular consensus that says the Spider's dramatic lines are, in fact, *enhanced* by the addition of a windscreen, the shape being better balanced in profile as a result, the truth is that it's the driving experience alone that maketh this car. And that remains as pure and unfettered by the swap to right-hand drive behind a looking glass as it would be by the driver changing underwear.

Venue for my first UK Renault Sport Spider encounter is the historic Goodwood motor racing circuit in Sussex on the south coast of England. Beneath a leaden sky and with a stiff wind blowing, directly from Siberia seemingly (spot the pattern emerging), I get to tour around a track layout that would have been familiar to Moss, Fangio and their ilk when this venue played host to the British Grand Prix best part of half a century ago.

It's a thrill, but since we have only a short time I concentrate on getting re-acquainted with the car rather than indulging in high-speed lappery and besides, this is the circuit that claimed the life of Bruce McLaren and finished the career of Stirling Moss - so I figure discretion should be the better part of valour. Particularly in a car that's the UK's one and only at the time of writing...

Next stop the Earl of March's Goodwood House and the instantly recognisable tree-lined driveway that plays host to the annual Festival of Speed. Again I resist the urge to go play, crossing the faded start line at a gentle jog rather than in the customary clutch-popping, engine screaming launch mode. And why not? For now I'm coming to appreciate the remarkably pliant low-speed ride, the bags of torque the powerplant provides that allows comfortable, burbling progress and - for the first time - I can watch the world go by from a Spider without the isolated, encapsulated feeling that

DRIVING THE SPIDER

comes with being enclosed in a crash helmet. Protected from the worst of the cold and the turbulence by the windscreen to the fore it may be chilly but it's most certainly invigorating. My therapist's services are no longer required!

And nor are those of the photographer - my all-too-brief drive can now begin in earnest. Except so, too, does the rain: spotting that all-important screen almost exactly on cue. To stop or not to stop, that is the question. As if...

I'm away to the hills - up and past the Glorious Goodwood racecourse with the wind in my hair but no rain: that gets deflected up over me by the glass up front and then tossed away, unwanted. Does this super new windscreen make the car UK user-friendly, even in the dripping, barren November countryside? By cringe you'd better believe it! This is no rolling panorama on a cinema screen but the South Downs alive and kicking in winter monochrome, punctuated by a flash of yellow and a red-nosed lunatic...

Am I carried away? Or should I be, by the men offering a smart new white coat with no buttons? No doubt: the Renault Sport Spider is no mere roadster pastiche of bygone areas but a living, breathing sports car entity born of the new millennium. It's for now. There are no art deco bits, no 'classic brand hallmarks', just something new, exciting and different. I don't want one. I need one. Right now. Please...

what the PAPERS say

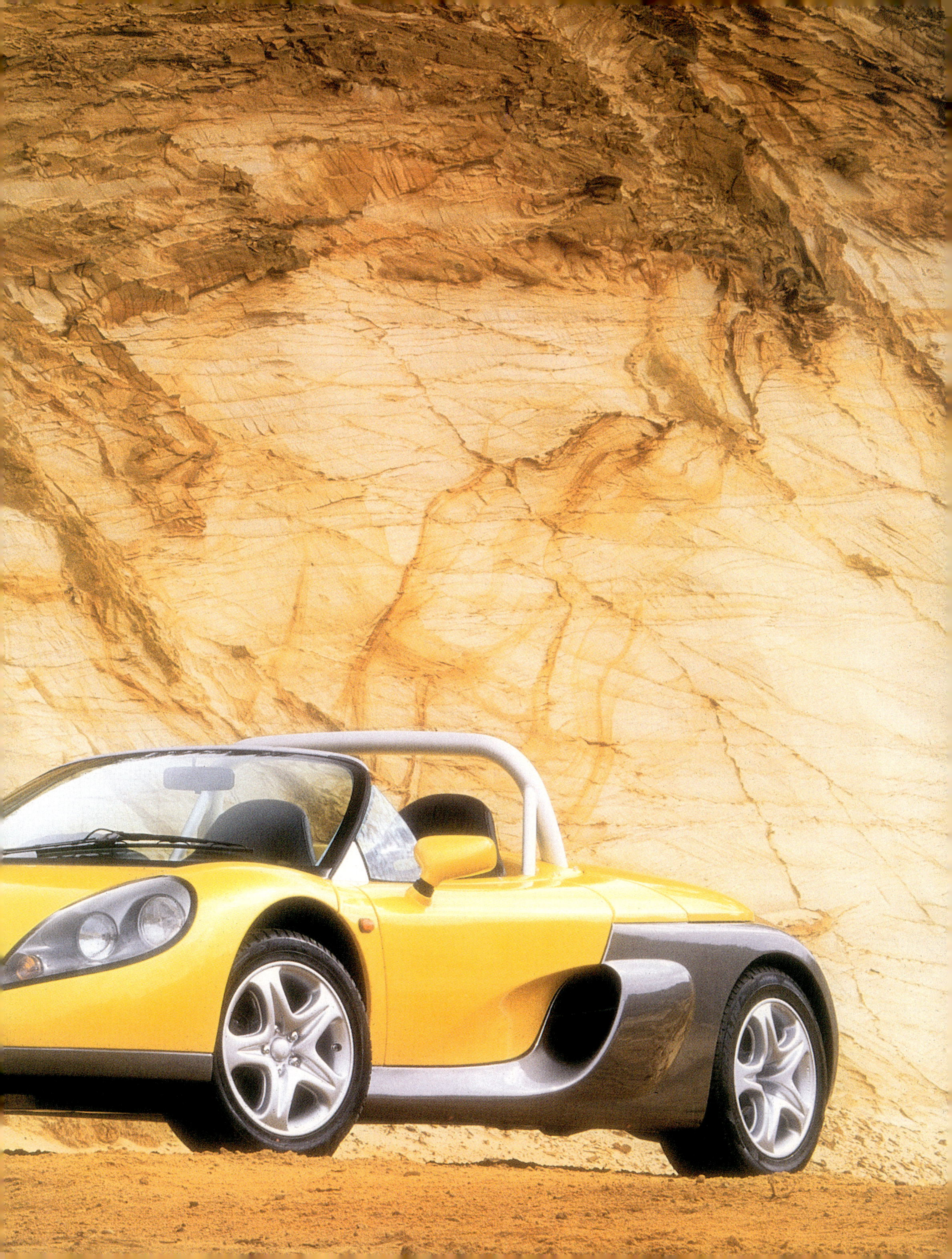

WHAT THE PAPERS SAY

"Although inspired by the Lancia Stratos, Ferrari Dino and Lotus Seven, there is nothing retrogressive about the Spider's aluminium chassis or attention-grabbing bodywork, fashioned in composite polyester. Its suspension, brakes and 150 horsepower 2.0-litre twin-cam engine (lifted straight from the Clio Williams) are bang up to date, too.

"Phenomenal handling, cornering and braking make it swift and entertaining, steering is supersensitive and uncorrupted by power assistance. Ditto the heavy brakes, while metal-to-metal suspension joints provide the sort of tactile feedback normally found only in karts and racing cars."
Roger Bell, *The Independent*

"The Spider's creators have followed the Lotus Seven concept - which means their car is simple and single-mindedly aimed at bare-teeth driving pleasure.

"The door opens upwards, scissor-style. It's light but strong and you do the usual supercar stretch over a wide aluminium-beam sill, before plopping down into the shell-seat. There's heaps of room in the cabin and the footwells are wide.

"The cabin is beautifully wrought, a striking combination of undisguised purpose, with visible aluminium chassis and designer-shaping for the body-coloured panelling.

"The throttle linkage is perfect: long in travel and deliciously snag-free, and when driving the Spider you're surrounded by a lot of car, especially widthways. It's broad and chunky.

"But once you're in the groove with the Spider its comportment is remarkable. Like all the best French cars it just isn't bothered by a less than perfect road surface. There's a fluency to the way it sails down a lumpy stretch. And not only can it shrug off bumps without getting thrown off the cornering line but it hardly troubles your comfort either. For a car with no rubber in the suspension the quality of the ride and its quietness are astonishing.

"The tyres, 205-section at the front and 225 behind, both on 16-inch wheels, cling on with an eye-popping doggedness - all told, the Spider transmits most of its info through the seat of your pants."
Paul Horrell, *Car*

"Stab the Spider's aluminium throttle pedal all the way to the floor, hear the high revving wail of the mid-mounted engine right behind and there's no mistaking it - this is a thinly disguised racing car with styling that's completely hat-stand!

"It's obviously nothing like any other car that's been seen before either, because driving the Spider has eyes widening, people falling off ladders, ice-creams dropping and bicycles crashing everywhere. Every street scene comes to a complete standstill as Renault's racer rolls beneath the disbelieving gazes of onlookers and other drivers.

"The first few corners are a revelation: no roll, but no understeer either, and with such a docile, revvy engine, no tail sliding as you power out - just fast, neutral cornering. A few more miles and you're pitching the car in at lunatic speeds and still it doesn't budge.

"Despite the fact that this car is less practical than a push-

WHAT THE PAPERS SAY

Above: UK journalists encounter Spider for the first time on the international press launch.

bike it's so original, so pure, so audacious and such a gas that Renault won't have a problem getting them out of showrooms."
Mark Walton, *Performance Car*

"A bike-quality view of the road ahead and the most direct steering you could possibly wish for elicit insect-ready teeth within the first hundred yards. Better yet, the Spider corners as flat as a freshly-steamrollered hedgehog whilst the ride remains remarkably forgiving.

"This has got to be the closest thing to biking available on four wheels. So immediate is your relationship with the road that the car becomes entirely secondary to the senses. Your only concern becomes speed over the ground and tackling the next twisty bit. And here's the secret of the Spider's abilities; it's essentially a racing car adapted for road use, rather than the all-too-common opposite."
Antony ffrench-Constant, *Top Gear*

"A single-seater for two? A motor cycle with four wheels? An escapee from a fairground? No, it's the Renault Sport Spider and die-hard sports-car enthusiasts will love its purity, originality and wonderfully communicative race-bred reflexes."
Tony Lewin, *The European*

"The Spider didn't merely look like a road racer, it had the hardwear to back it up. This car's handling is extraordinary: adhesion levels are those of the very best supercars yet the ride quality is brilliantly supple and comfortable - and it will corner like a Ferrari F355..."
Andrew Frankel, *Autosport*

"The Spider has the body of a 21st-century racing car and the technology to match."
Ray Massey, *Daily Mail*

"There is a seminal bit in *Zen and the Art of Motor Cycle Maintenance* where Robert Pirsig talks about the essential distinctions between riding a motor bike and driving a car. It goes as follows.

"You see things vacationing on a motor cycle in a way that is completely different to any other. In a car you're always in a compartment and, because you're used to it, you don't realise that through the car window everything you see is just more TV. You're a passive observer and it's all moving by you boringly in a frame.

"On a cycle the frame is gone. You're completely in contact with it all. You're in the scene, not just watching it any more, and the sense of presence is overwhelming. That concrete whizzing by five inches beneath your foot is the real thing, the same stuff you walk on. It's right there, so blurred you can't focus on it, yet you can put your foot down and touch it any time - and the whole

WHAT THE PAPERS SAY

thing, the whole experience, is never removed from the immediate consciousness."

"It's a lot like that when you drive the Renault Sport Spider - you sit there with the scenery coming directly at you. But it's also in its very soul. The Spider is an outlandish race-car for the road and, with its manically screaming engine, instant responsiveness and zero concession to luxury, it has a direct, involving, real feel that is part bike, part car.

"Imagine a Caterham Seven without the demanding nervousness, the ludicrously difficult entry and exit or the uncomfortable cramped cockpit. That's the Renault Sport Spider...

"It's an extraordinary-looking thing, futuristic beyond belief when you set your eyes on it in the flesh, even though the way the front end meets the road is reminiscent of the Alpine-Renault A110.

"Some day, when we have devised less problematical ways of getting from A to B, cars will become mere toys for committed enthusiasts. And those cars will be just like the Renault Sport Spider: uncompromised pleasure."
Mark Felton, *Motoring News*

"The Spider's a pure fun car with beautifully balanced handling and responds to steering input as sharply as a go-kart."
Ken Rogers, *Daily Mirror*

"The Spider should, by all conventions, never have been built. Car makers show concept models like it all the time at motor shows claiming they are the future - then go off and make something that looks as interesting as a milk-float. Renault actually did it with the Spider, making a car quite unlike anything else - it's one of the most remarkable shapes to come out of any car factory."
Kevin Eason, *The Times*

"The Renault Sport Spider is as close as most motorists will ever get to driving a real racing car - it's fast, fun and flashy..."
David Williams, *Daily Express*

"The Spider is a four-wheeled motor cycle for a blast on a sunny day or racing at the weekends. It has sharp responses and precise handling - a very 'pure' driving experience, akin to mid-engined racing cars of a few years' back. You can pay more for much less fun..."
Ray Hutton, *The Sunday Times*

"The Spider's lines are extraordinary, as mindful of the future as the Caterham Seven is of the past and breathtakingly appealing, too. As you climb aboard every sign is encouraging. Step over the sill and your eyes are drawn to the naked aluminium chassis. There are no carpets, just drilled (and adjustable) pedals, thin racing bucket seats and an instrumental binnacle dead ahead that's notable for its lack of speedometer.

"Aluminium is not restricted to the structure either; it's allowed to play right around the cabin with bare metal forming the dashboard, grab handles and gearstick. It's a

WHAT THE PAPERS SAY

great interior to look at.

"The reaction at the front wheels is that of a racing car. Yet this does not bring unacceptable nervousness or a crashing ride. Quite the reverse in fact; the Spider merely feels data-logged into your brain while the ride quality is eerily impressive.

"The first corner: hard on the brakes, note sublime pedal feel, ideal weighting and bizarre deceleration...

"The grip is stupendous. Wearing Michelin Pilot tyres the Spider dives into the apex, steering flooded with feel, carrying every available scrap of momentum on to the next straight. You'd need a Ferrari F355 before you found another car which would even think of cornering so hard.

"Driving harder now I find I have so far discovered but a fraction of the chassis's extraordinary talents. Each corner is a joyous blend of race car grip and response, yet with none of the associated nervousness. You can hit bumps and huge potholes, ride surface and camber changes and the Spider just copes. You can even trail brake into the apex, challenging its grip at the rear, and the car will kill the mild understeer that is the handling's ultimate steady-state default setting before, if you know when, allowing its tail to slip briefly out of line on a kick of throttle.

"What Renault has created is a hugely fresh and attractive road racer with some genuinely awesome dynamics. It is a wondrous car that has provided some of the more memorable minutes of my motoring life to date. And I am almost beside myself with admiration that such a sprawling corporation has had the balls to decide to create such a no-nonsense driver's car, and the ability then to make one."
Andrew Frankel, *Autocar*

"The Renault Sport Spider is the most sensational-looking car of 1996. Forget Alfa's Spyder, BMW's James Bond Z3, Mercedes' SLK or even the brilliant Lotus Elise. When it comes to heavenly bodies this French flier is the traffic-stopper of the year.

"And what's a bit of cold when a car looks drop-dead gorgeous and is almost as much fun to drive as look at - it sticks to the road with all the grip you'd expect from its Renault racing pedigree...

"If you can afford one, buy it."
Ken Gibson, *The Sun*

"Jumping from design board to tarmac in just fifteen months, this road racer is a raw, minimalist machine with a rear-wheel drive, rear-engined layout - just like a Porsche 911.

"And what a body! No matter where I went with 'my' Spider crowds gathered and heads spun. And this car may grab all the attention on crowded urban streets, but it's on the open road that it really sizzles. On hilly hairpin roads I couldn't stop grinning as it worked its magic, flowing through bends with plenty of grip at both ends.

"What you need is there and nothing else, which is the way it should be in a car with such a focused role. Those who nab a Spider will have a future classic..."
James Mills, *Auto Express*

a question of SPORT

Services
elf
elf
SODICAM
Philips Car Systems
MICHELIN
elf ULTIMATE OIL
SODICAM

A QUESTION OF SPORT

Given that it was Renault Sport's Christian Contzen who instigated the whole Spider project, with a view to using the car for a one-make race series, it comes as little surprise to find that the race specification and road specification cars are so very, very similar. Buy a Renault Sport Spider for the road and you are getting an undiluted race car for your money, not some half-baked King's Road cruiser that could take a roll-cage at a push.

Conversely, go racing in a Spider and there's no mistaking that this is the real thing: there is clear evidence of Renault Sport's race-bred expertise running right through the car. From its lightweight construction, sophisticated suspension plus steering and braking responses that are akin to a single seater, it is obvious that the Spider is born to run - and therein lies much of the appeal: this is not a car that flatters to deceive.

Created for use in both a pan-European series (the Spider Eurocup) and a dedicated UK competition (the *Elf Renault Sport Spider UK Cup*), the racing version of the Renault Sport Spider is pretty well just as the road car described elsewhere. The low, squat lines are nigh unhindered, save for the addition of a (good looking) 'web-style' safety roll-cage, and modifications are limited to those of a minor technical nature for improved performance and safety on circuit.

The Spider's basic structure is not only so light as to be ideal for racing but also exceptionally rigid, a major safety feature that's at least as important when competing as when pushing hard on country switchbacks. The Spider's bodyshell, moulded in polyester composite, also proves just what the race doctor ordered; again proving light yet strong.

Where the road car has a passenger seat the racer has a rigid tonneau cover, integral with the bodywork, while two cooling ducts are sited on the racer's rear bonnet cover to force air into the engine feed system and engine-oil cooling radiator. Two opaque headlight covers take the place of the road car's glass items.

In either guise the Spider's suspension and underpinnings are direct spin-offs of state-of-the-art motor racing technology. The front suspension combines double wishbones and rigidly-mounted ball joints, with no rubber engine mounts and, unusually, the double wishbones at the rear are rotated ninety degrees. The lower ball joints mounted on the hub carriers are in line with the horizontal wheel axis and set very low down, so as to bear load as close to the ground as possible.

The other unique feature of the rear axle is that the upper wishbones directly control the spring/damper unit and the anti-roll bar via vertical tie-rods.

The hubs of the Renault Sport Spider are derived from the late Alpine A610 supercar, as are the callipers and the three hundred-millimetre diameter ventilated brake discs. That's braking capacity designed for a car of some 1400kg in a car weighing well under 1000kg!

Located just behind the gearlever, what's more, is a control that allows the driver to vary braking distribution and to choose optimal braking efficiency under race conditions. It's yet another example of the attention to detail and the purity of the driving experience the Spider offers.

Spider race and road wheels are of the same dimensions: sixteen inch diameter wheels, eight inch rims at the front, nine inches at the rear. Michelin supply two types for competition - treaded for use in wet conditions and slicks for use in the dry. They help to get the most out of the car's dynamic behaviour no matter what the state of the circuit.

The output of the race-specification two-litre, sixteen-valve engine is boosted

A QUESTION OF SPORT

from the already quick standard car's 150bhp at 6000rpm to around 180bhp at 7200rpm, through the use of two new camshafts and a specially-developed electronic control unit. The engine's optimised torque has also been increased, to a little over 151lbs/ft at 5400rpm from 136lbs/ft at the same engine speed, while a new exhaust system has been specially-designed to cope with this improved performance.

Ditto the gearbox, derived from the Clio racers of old, a *six*-speed unit (the roadgoing Spider has five speeds) for track use that uses a dog engagement rather than synchromesh - in common with all serious race cars.

What does all of this translate to? In bare figures: maximum speed rises from 134mph to 136mph, the 0-62mph benchmark sprint time drops from 6.9 seconds to 6.2 seconds and the standing kilometre from 27.5 seconds to 26 seconds exactly. From quick to even quicker...

And just so the racer is complete, the finishing touches: in goes the requisite six-point safety harness (the seats on the road car can accommodate that, too) along with a digital dashboard from the Formula Renault Sport single-seater racing car. It provides the driver with vital race data through its rev-counter, water temperature and oil pressure indicators - and now the Renault Sport Spider is ready for the grid...

So what happens next? Thrills and spills galore, that's what! See for yourself: here follows the diary of the inaugural *Elf* Renault Sport Spider UK Cup season that saw the brilliant Jason Plato crowned 1996 champion driver...

SEASON DIARY

PLATO WINS FIRST SPIDER ENCOUNTER

Brands Hatch, 21st April 1996

Jason Plato won the first ever Elf Renault Sport Spider UK Cup race. Starting from sixth on the grid he flew past three other contenders in his Swan National Spider to take third place by the end of the first lap. He took second place from Paula Cook a lap later then the lead from Scott Lakin on lap three and, after shaking off the attentions of second placed Julian Westwood, simply dominated the remainder of the twenty-lap race. A jubilant Plato said afterwards:

"I had a good start and after the first couple of laps it was pretty much plain sailing. The cars are great fun to drive, you can get sideways with them but still go quickly. It was brilliant to win the first race of a new championship but now I've got to keep doing a job if I'm going to be a title contender."

Orbit Motorsport's Westwood started fourth and slotted in behind Plato on the second lap. The duo passed *Renault Retail Group*'s Scott Lakin on lap three and Westwood then

SEASON DIARY

began to challenge Plato for the lead.

"I didn't get a good start off the line," rued Westwood, "and on the first lap I fought hard with the slower cars in front of me. Jason and I got past Scott at Druids but, as he got through first, Jason was able to break away. I chased him hard for a few laps but after having a big moment at Paddock Hill Bend I decided I couldn't catch up and so settled for second place and the valuable points."

Formula Three driver Paula Cook made a one-off appearance in her team's Spider and provided a spirited performance from start to finish. Having held second place to Lakin on the first lap she dropped down to fourth behind the charging Plato and Westwood. On lap fourteen she nipped past Lakin, though, and finished on the podium in third position.

"I'm really happy with the result considering I only drove the car for the first time on Wednesday," she said. "Scott and I had a good battle towards the end after Jason got past me at Paddock Hill Bend and I didn't even see Julian! I enjoyed the race, though, and the car is certainly very different to what I'm used to."

The starting line-up was reshuffled for the fastest eight drivers after qualifying due to the new ballot rule - they drew lots to determine their grid positions for the race. It meant that the likes of Jason Plato, who set the fastest time in qualifying, didn't actually start from pole but had to fight up from sixth.

Behind early leader Lakin in fifth place came David Shaw, shaping up to be a serious contender for the championship. Shaw began the race at the back of the grid after a shunt in practice and blazed through the field to pass Redgrave Racing's Sean McNally for fifth on the penultimate lap. David won the *Mintex* Driver of the Day as a result of overtaking twelve cars during the race.

Grant Elliott driving his *Slick 50* Spider, *Bison Clothing*-sponsored Russell Morgan and Last Engineering's Andy Wolfe all provided spirited performances from start to finish as the trio chased each other for a top ten slot. Elliott came out on top to come home seventh followed by Morgan and Wolfe. Greg Hart drove his *Elf* Spider to ninth on the road but a jump start meant he was given a ten second penalty which dropped him to eleventh place behind GT Services' Rowland Bratt.

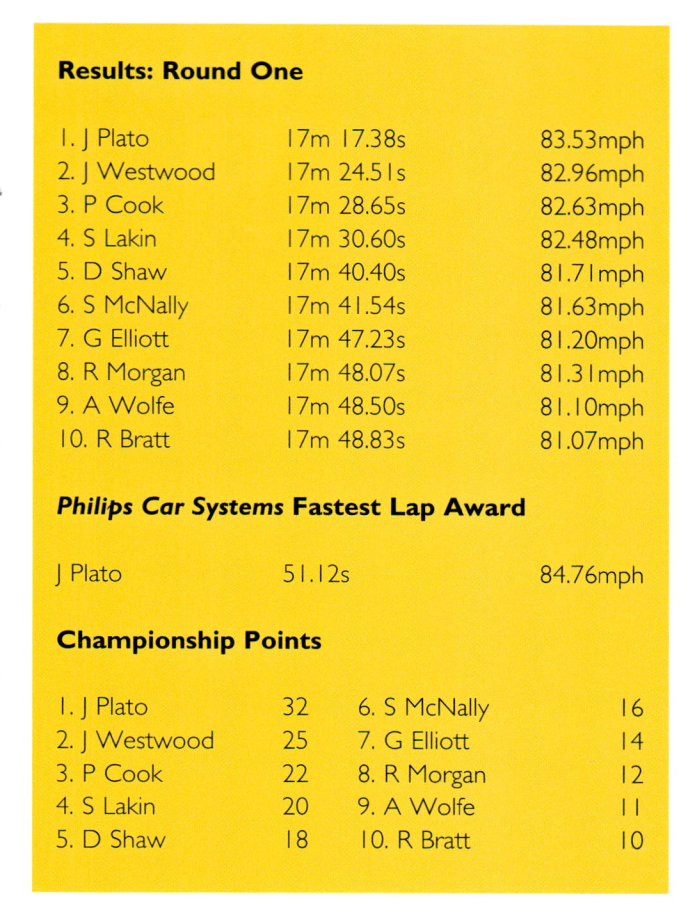

Morgan Walker Racing's Howard Walker held eighth position early on but he spun at Paddock Hill Bend on lap eleven, which dropped him to seventeenth place. He recovered to pass Kiwi Nigel Arkell and Dave Cox to finish a creditable twelfth.

Results: Round One

1. J Plato	17m 17.38s	83.53mph
2. J Westwood	17m 24.51s	82.96mph
3. P Cook	17m 28.65s	82.63mph
4. S Lakin	17m 30.60s	82.48mph
5. D Shaw	17m 40.40s	81.71mph
6. S McNally	17m 41.54s	81.63mph
7. G Elliott	17m 47.23s	81.20mph
8. R Morgan	17m 48.07s	81.31mph
9. A Wolfe	17m 48.50s	81.10mph
10. R Bratt	17m 48.83s	81.07mph

Philips Car Systems Fastest Lap Award

J Plato	51.12s	84.76mph

Championship Points

1. J Plato	32	6. S McNally	16
2. J Westwood	25	7. G Elliott	14
3. P Cook	22	8. R Morgan	12
4. S Lakin	20	9. A Wolfe	11
5. D Shaw	18	10. R Bratt	10

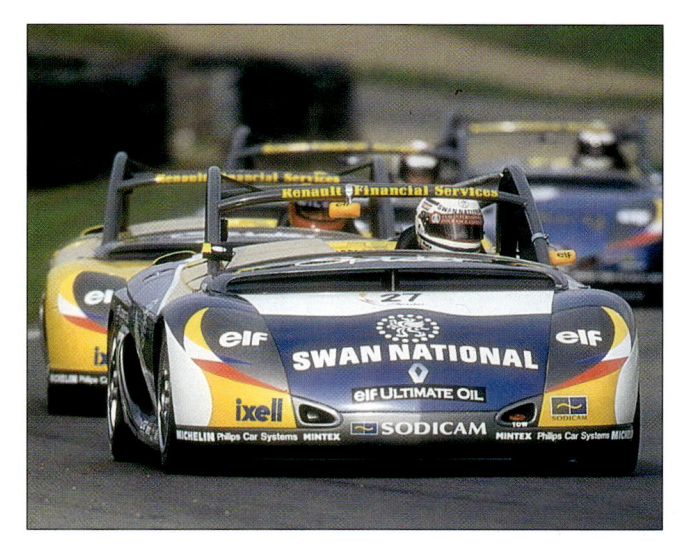

SEASON DIARY

PLATO MAKES IT TWO IN A ROW

Thruxton, 6th May 1996

Championship leader Jason Plato won his second consecutive round of the Elf Renault Sport Spider UK Cup - but needed some help from Lady Luck. The race was stopped after two laps when Jason was lying a distant third but after the re-start of the shortened seven-lap race Plato made a clean get away into a lead he held from start to finish. He said later:

"It was a shame the first race was stopped in a way but it enabled me to make a better second start. Then my main objective on the first lap was to make no mistakes and gain as much distance over Julian Westwood as possible. Obviously it's important to do well at the first couple of rounds and so far I have done that - I'm certainly looking forward to Silverstone..."

Julian Westwood took the chequered flag behind Plato having pursued him until the fifth lap when he admitted giving up the chase. The front-runner, whose team Orbit Motorsport had earlier won the *Sodicam/Ixell* Best Presented Team, commented:

"This round was certainly closer than Brands where Jason had the edge. I managed to close on him once or twice but decided to call it a day because the gap was just too great. I'm very happy with my car's set-up and a few more points in the bag is clearly a good thing."

Scott Lakin had his first podium finish this season when he took third place driving his *Renault Retail Group* Spider: "I made a good start but missed a gear which let Jason through and the same thing happened again a few laps later at Goodwood Corner, when Westwood was able to pass. The car itself is a handful which makes the racing interesting and I'm pleased I got the extra points."

Top Gear Motorsport presenter Tiff Needell made a guest appearance driving DC Cook Racing's Spider and finished a commendable fourth, despite constant pressure from Sean McNally. Tiff squeezed ahead of McNally on the opening lap but Sean drove his *Allsport Management* Spider hard and regained fourth position on lap four. Tiff was then hot on his heels, the pair enjoying a cracking duel until Needell nipped past at the final corner to finish fourth. Said Tiff:

"I had an excellent battle with Sean and thought I'd leave the overtaking for the Grandstand! The car was wonderful and great fun to drive."

Redgrave Racing's McNally had an identical result to his brother Rollo who finished fifth in the preceding *Ultrafilter International*

Results: Round Two

1. J Plato	10m 13.04s	96.84mph
2. J Westwood	10m 15.07s	96.52mph
3. S Lakin	10m 16.12s	96.36mph
4. T Needell	10m 24.17s	95.12mph
5. S McNally	10m 24.80s	95.02mph
6. B Wilson	10m 27.83s	94.56mph
7. D Shaw	10m 30.94s	94.09mph
8. G Hart	10m 31.51s	94.01mph
9. D Cox	10m 32.91s	93.80mph
10. G Elliott	10m 34.07s	93.63mph

Philips Car Systems Fastest Lap Award

J Westwood	1m 26.08s	98.53mph

Championship Points

1. J Plato	62		6. G Elliott	24
2. J Westwood	52		7. P Cook	22
3. S Lakin	42		8. G Hart	21
4. S McNally	34		9. T Needell	20
5. D Shaw	32		9. A Wolfe	20

SEASON DIARY

Formula Renault Sport race. Sean, who was awarded the *Mintex* Driver of the Day for his performance, commented: "Tiff passed me on the hill going into the last corner; I went to go on the inside then outside but I couldn't get through. All in all it was a good race though."

Another entertaining battle came from Bryce Wilson and David Shaw. It started when Shaw, driving his *Riverside Medical* Spider flew past Wilson on lap five. Bryce continued to hound David and robbed him of sixth place on the final lap. Bryce was well pleased: "I missed a gear on the first lap and the pack got away but I managed to recover to give David a run for his money. Overall, I feel I still need to adjust to the car but I'm pleased with the way things went."

London's Greg Hart qualified on the fourth row but due to a poor start dropped to eighth behind David Shaw on the opening lap which he maintained until the chequered flag. Following eighth-placed Hart were Dave Cox and Grant Elliott who completed the top ten.

SEASON DIARY

PLATO HOLDS ON FOR A HAT-TRICK

Silverstone, 19th May 1996

Jason Plato continued his perfect start to the season when he completed a hat-trick by winning the third round of the Elf Renault Sport Spider UK Cup in damp track conditions.

Plato made the most of his *Philips Car Systems* pole position to lead the race from start to finish, but it was the hardest win of his three, coming under attack from Julian Westwood in the closing laps and defending his slender lead right up to the last corner. Jason commented:

"It was a tough race and if it had gone on for another lap I would have been in big trouble as I just don't think I could have held Julian off."

Orbit Motorsport's Julian Westwood came second despite starting the race from the back of the grid due to a gearbox problem in qualifying. Westwood drove his Renault Spider hard on the first lap making up a staggering *ten* places. After a short battle with *Renault Retail Group's* Scott Lakin for fourth place on lap two, he passed Sean McNally at Becketts Corner and then David Shaw at Luffield on the same lap to move into second place.

On the final lap 27 year-old Westwood was close enough to the leader to make a final lunge for glory but, although he hounded Plato at Priory and

SEASON DIARY

Brooklands corners, he was unable to pass him and finished second. The *Mintex* Driver of the Day winner said afterwards:

"I had a good start and the drivers at the back of the field were helpful in letting me pass them. I was so close to Jason on the last lap but he played it perfectly. I gave him a nudge and went on the outside at Woodcote Corner but he's no fool, he knew what I was doing and I couldn't pass him!"

David Shaw came in behind Westwood, taking his first podium finish of the season. Shaw took his *Riverside Medical* Spider into third on the first lap and two laps later moved to second. However, Westwood robbed him of second place and left Shaw to spend the remainder of the race fighting off the attentions of Redgrave Racing's Sean McNally and Ian Cantwell. Said Shaw: "I didn't have a particularly good start and then all of a sudden Julian was behind me. I missed a few gears which gave him the chance to pass me though I'm glad of a podium finish - hopefully I'll now be up there a lot more from now on."

Former touring car racer Ian Cantwell had an impressive drive in his second race of the championship - starting the race from eighth and finishing fourth. Cantwell had a bad start, what's more, and dropped four places to twelfth on the opening lap, but by lap six he had crept up to ninth and had an entertaining battle with Lakin and David Cox for sixth position. On lap seven he challenged Bryce Wilson for fifth and, after passing him, went on to put McNally under intense pressure for fourth. Come the final lap McNally gave in to the attack allowing Cantwell past. Cantwell, who won both the *Mintex* Driver of the Day and *Sodicam/Ixell* Best Prepared Team Award enthused:

"My main aim in the first half of the race, due to the wet conditions, was to stay on the track - but as soon as it dried up I started to push harder. I'm happy with today's result, my aim is to keep moving up."

Sean McNally had a disappointing third round as, despite having started the race on the front row of the grid, he finished fifth: "The first half of the race went well. I had a reasonable start and was trying to stay behind Plato but David and Julian passed me. In the end I lost fourth to Ian, too, which I am annoyed about…"

Andy Wolfe made a good start from twelfth and rose six places to finish sixth, taking his first ever fastest lap in a Renault event. He was followed by Morgan Walker Racing's Bryce Wilson who, at one point, was in fifth position but finished seventh. Wilson commented: "If I could do the race again I would have chosen different settings

Results: Round Three

1. J Plato	17m 34.45s	75.73mph
2. J Westwood	17m 34.68s	75.71mph
3. D Shaw	17m 40.58s	75.29mph
4. I Cantwell	17m 48.36s	74.74mph
5. S McNally	17m 48.98s	74.63mph
6. A Wolfe	17m 51.80s	74.50mph
7. B Wilson	18m 00.03s	73.94mph
8. D Cox	18m 06.69s	73.48mph
9. S Lakin	18m 07.71s	73.41mph
10. S Maddison	18m 12.09s	73.12mph

Philips Car Systems Fastest Lap Award

A Wolfe	1m 39.79s	79.90mph

Championship Points

1. J Plato	92	6. A Wolfe	36
2. J Westwood	77	7. G Elliott	33
3. D Shaw	54	8. B Wilson	30
4. S Lakin	53	9. D Cox	26
5. S McNally	52	10. I Cantwell	23

on the car. The conditions made the race difficult and I was just trying to hang in there - it was tough."

Dave Cox started on the second row but dropped to finish the race in eighth. Cox was followed by 25 year-old Scott Lakin who suffered severely due to the fact that his Menu Motorsport Spider was "too stiff, the car was set up wrong." Lakin started the race fifth on the grid and slowly dropped down the pack.

Tollbar Racing's Sam Maddison scored his first top ten finish of the season late on. Maddison was working with Lotus Global GT driver Perry McCarthy when he tested at the circuit on Thursday and the improvements to his Spider's set-up paid dividends in Sunday's race.

SEASON DIARY

FOUR OUT OF FOUR FOR PLATO

Oulton Park, 27th May 1996

Championship leader Jason Plato stormed through from seventh to first in just three laps on his way to taking his fourth consecutive Elf Renault Sport Spider UK Cup win in damp weather conditions.

Swan National's Plato drove his Spider hard in the early laps and, after a short battle with Bryce Wilson for third place, he went on to challenge Scott Lakin for second. Menu Motorsport's Lakin spun on lap two which allowed Plato to put pressure on leader David Shaw and, by the end of the third lap, Jason had snatched the lead and went on to win by a comfortable two-second margin. Said the 27 year old:

"I made a fabulous start and knew I had made the right choice, using wet tyres, as the track was pretty slippery. The car handled exactly as I thought it would and once I got into the lead I stretched my legs and cruised on to take the chequered flag."

Shaw secured his highest finish of the season, making a good start from pole position to lead the opening laps, but had to fight off advances from Lakin and Ben Edwards. Shaw commented: "I had a difficult start because when you are at the front it's hard to tell how much grip you've got. Jason overtook me at Island Bend and, after trying to keep up with him, I swapped my attentions to fending off Ben."

Eurosport television commentator Ben Edwards drove an exceptional debut Spider race, finishing third and winning one of the two *Mintex* Driver of the Day Awards. Edwards started from the second row in his DC Cook Racing-entered Spider and by lap five had overtaken Lakin and Wilson moving into third. Morgan Walker Motorsport's Wilson was hot on his heels throughout the race in what became a three-way battle between Edwards, Wilson and Lakin. Edwards said afterwards:

"It was good fun. Obviously I'm very happy with the result and throughout the race my aim was to pass Bryce and get away from his battle with Scott. Later, I saw a chance to catch David in the closing laps but I didn't want to do anything silly so I settled for third."

Renault Retail Group-sponsored Scott Lakin won the *Philips Car Systems* Fastest Lap Award but had a mixed race. He made a good start going into the lead by Old Hall Corner but he spun on the second lap at Knickerbrook, dropping to sixth. After moving back into fifth Lakin put pressure on Wilson for fourth place and for the remainder of the race Scott fought hard with Bryce but couldn't overtake. Although on the road Wilson finished fourth, his car failed post-race scrutineering and he was disqualified.

Ian Cantwell stormed to fifth place having started from eighth on the grid. JRC Motorsport's Cantwell, who initially fought with Russell Morgan and later Scott Lakin, said: "I didn't really push the

SEASON DIARY

car as hard as I could have done because I haven't driven the car in the wet before - I was basically trying to stay on the track." On the road Russell Morgan finished fifth but he was given a twenty-second penalty when he missed the Knickerbrook chicane twice, dropping him to seventh.

Asquith Autosport's Grant Elliott was the other *Mintex* Driver of the Day after qualifying in twelfth position and finishing sixth in his *Slick 50*-backed Spider. Elliott looked as though he was catching up with Cantwell towards the end of the ten-lap race and crossed the finish line just a second adrift. Grant said: "I thought I was in with a chance to pass Ian but I couldn't get close enough - I'm happy with the result though."

Last Engineering's Andy Wolfe started twelfth on the grid and made up four places by the end of the race to finish eighth. Wolfe is currently sixth in the championship and said: "I had a blinding start but nearly spun at Cascades which worried me a bit. All in all I had a pretty lonely race."

Julian Westwood is currently second in the championship, however, he had a disappointing race to finish ninth after choosing to use dry as opposed to wet weather tyres - which in the damp conditions failed to give him enough traction. Menu Motorsport's Mark Donkersley secured his first top ten finish of the season.

The *Sodicam/Ixell* Best Prepared Team Award went to Tollbar Racing.

Results: Round Four

1. J Plato	20m 42.10s	80.42mph
2. D Shaw	20m 45.01s	80.24mph
3. B Edwards	20m 45.51s	80.20mph
4. S Lakin	20m 45.51s	79.46mph
5. I Cantwell	20m 58.23s	79.39mph
6. G Elliott	20m 59.25s	79.33mph
7. R Morgan	21m 16.81s	78.24mph
8. A Wolfe	21m 20.77s	77.99mph
9. J Westwood	21m 20.82s	77.99mph
10. M Donkersley	21m 24.98s	77.74mph

Philips Car Systems Fastest Lap Award

S Lakin	2m 02.30s	81.68mph

Championship Points

1. J Plato	122		6. A Wolfe	48
2. J Westwood	88		7. G Elliott	49
3. D Shaw	79		8. I Cantwell	41
4. S Lakin	75		9. B Wilson	30
5. S McNally	52		10. R Morgan	29

SEASON DIARY

TAKE FIVE FOR PLATO

Snetterton, 16th June 1996

Jason Plato took his fifth consecutive win of the season at Snetterton circuit in the Elf Renault Sport Spider UK Cup. Plato blazed through the field from third on the grid taking the lead just before Riches Corner on lap one and was never headed for the remaining laps.

In his *Swan National*-sponsored Spider he pushed hard as he was being shadowed by Julian Westwood for the first ten laps of the race. He said: "I had a cracking start and took the lead just before Riches. The car's clutch went on the second lap but thankfully I still managed to stay ahead of Julian."

Pole-sitter Westwood finished second and gave Plato a run for his money for the majority of the fifteen-lap race. He set the fastest lap time on the tenth lap, winning him the *Philips Car Systems* Fastest Lap Award, but his luck ran out a lap later when his *Datamatic*-sponsored Spider went onto the grass at the Esses enabling Jason to increase his lead. Westwood commented:

"I tried very hard to catch up with Jason after I went onto the grass but I just could not get close enough to pass him. I thought I could catch up at the breaking areas and, although I did, on the straights he was way ahead of me."

Evans Halshaw-backed David Shaw secured his third consecutive podium finish in coming home third. The 36 year-old started the race on the second row and went into fourth place on the opening lap. On the second lap *Renault*

SEASON DIARY

Retail Group-sponsored Scott Lakin passed David, demoting him to fifth, and then Morgan Walker Motorsport's Russell Morgan - who was in front of him - missed a gear enabling Shaw to regain fourth slot. David continued in fourth until Lakin pitted due to engine problems. He said: "I had a few slow laps but caught up with Scott half-way through the race. Obviously I am very pleased with today's results and I am glad for the points which strengthen my place in the championship."

Russell Morgan scored his highest finish of the season when notching a respectable fourth. The 34 year-old had a good start and sliced past his rivals from the third row on the grid into third place on the opening lap in his *Bison Clothes*-backed Spider. On lap two Morgan was overtaken by Scott Lakin, dropping him to fourth, and he came under attack from David Shaw who was hot on his heels in fifth place. Unfortunately Russell missed a gear allowing Shaw and Asquith Autosport's Grant Elliott to pass him on lap three.

By the fifth lap David Cox had overtaken Morgan and a three-way battle began between the pair and Andy Wolfe for sixth place. By the seventh lap 38 year-old Wolfe had retired and Russell's harrying paid off as he squeezed ahead of Cox. Scott Lakin's departure from the race moved the pack up and then Elliott spun out on the penultimate lap hounding Morgan - who finished in fourth place - winning him the *Mintex* Driver of the Day. He said: "I had an excellent start but missed a gear on the first lap causing me to lose places. I had a good battle with Grant and after he went out of the race I had a free run until the end." In fifth place came Mardi Gras Motorsport's Dave Cox in his *W.E Cox (Recoveries)*-liveried Spider.

The forty year-old secured his highest starting position in the championship this season at the Norfolk circuit but, although he started on the front row, he had a bad start which caused him to drop four places to sixth on the first lap. By lap seven Redgrave Racing's Sean McNally and Russell Morgan had nipped past him but Cox challenged McNally and re- claimed seventh place on lap eight. By the eleventh lap Dave was fighting off the attentions from Howard Walker but managed to keep him at bay until the chequered flag.

Walker scored his first top six finish of the season from tenth on the grid but dropped a place at the start before moving up one position on the second lap to begin a fierce battle with Greg Hart. Hart chased Walker hard but retired with gearbox problems on the seventh lap leaving Walker to challenge McNally for eighth place. By lap thirteen McNally had dropped three places leaving Walker sixth.

The fifth round of the *Elf* Renault Sport Spider UK Cup witnessed Alan Humberstone racing for the first time in over fifteen years and he finished a creditable seventh. Humberstone was also awarded the second *Mintex* Driver of the Day prize after the 39 year-old had an entertaining battle with Rowland Bratt from start to finish. He enthused: "The car is great fun to drive and I had a good time out there. It's great to be back racing again!"

Rowland Bratt crossed the line closely behind Humberstone in eighth place followed by Sean McNally in ninth and Dennis Bunning who completed the top ten.

The *Sodicam/Ixell* Best Prepared Team Award went to Asquith Autosport.

Results: Round Five

1. J Plato	20m 13.34s	86.87mph
2. J Westwood	20m 16.51s	86.64mph
3. D Shaw	20m 23.15s	86.17mph
4. R Morgan	20m 41.70s	84.89mph
5. D Cox	20m 47.88s	84.46mph
6. H Walker	20m 53.69s	84.07mph
7. A Humberstone	21m 04.58s	83.35mph
8. R Bratt	21m 05.66s	83.28mph
9. S McNally	21m 10.11s	82.99mph
10. D Bunning (behind 1 lap)	21m 20.31s	80.61mph

Philips Car Systems Fastest Lap Award

J Westwood	1m 19.47s	88.42mph

Championship Points

1. J Plato	152		6. G Elliott	49
2. J Westwood	115		6. R Morgan	49
3. D Shaw	101		8. A Wolfe	48
4. S Lakin	75		9. D Cox	44
5. S McNally	63		10. I Cantwell	41